This Bucket List Planner Belongs
To:

Bucket List

Date Completed

What I Want To Do:

BUCKET LIST ITEM: #

THOUGHTS & REFLECTIONS

Bucket List

Date Completed

What I Want To Do:

BUCKET LIST ITEM: #

THOUGHTS & REFLECTIONS

Bucket List

Date Completed

What I Want To Do:

BUCKET LIST ITEM: #

THOUGHTS & REFLECTIONS

Bucket List

Date Completed

What I Want To Do:

BUCKET LIST ITEM: #

THOUGHTS & REFLECTIONS

Bucket List

What I Want To Do:

Date Completed

BUCKET LIST ITEM: #

THOUGHTS & REFLECTIONS

Bucket List

Date Completed

What I Want To Do:

BUCKET LIST ITEM: #

THOUGHTS & REFLECTIONS

Bucket List

Date Completed

What I Want To Do:

BUCKET LIST ITEM: #

THOUGHTS & REFLECTIONS

Bucket List

Date Completed

What I Want To Do:

BUCKET LIST ITEM: #

THOUGHTS & REFLECTIONS

Bucket List

Date Completed

What I Want To Do:

BUCKET LIST ITEM: #

THOUGHTS & REFLECTIONS

Bucket List

Date Completed

What I Want To Do:

BUCKET LIST ITEM: #

THOUGHTS & REFLECTIONS

Bucket List

Date Completed

What I Want To Do:

BUCKET LIST ITEM: #

THOUGHTS & REFLECTIONS

Bucket List

Date Completed

What I Want To Do:

BUCKET LIST ITEM: #

THOUGHTS & REFLECTIONS

Bucket List

Date Completed

What I Want To Do:

BUCKET LIST ITEM: #

THOUGHTS & REFLECTIONS

Bucket List

Date Completed

What I Want To Do:

BUCKET LIST ITEM: #

THOUGHTS & REFLECTIONS

Bucket List

Date Completed

What I Want To Do:

BUCKET LIST ITEM: #

THOUGHTS & REFLECTIONS

Bucket List

Date Completed

What I Want To Do:

BUCKET LIST ITEM: #

THOUGHTS & REFLECTIONS

Bucket List

Date Completed

What I Want To Do:

BUCKET LIST ITEM: #

THOUGHTS & REFLECTIONS

Bucket List

Date Completed

What I Want To Do:

BUCKET LIST ITEM: #

THOUGHTS & REFLECTIONS

Bucket List

Date Completed

What I Want To Do:

BUCKET LIST ITEM: #

THOUGHTS & REFLECTIONS

Bucket List

Date Completed

What I Want To Do:

BUCKET LIST ITEM: #

THOUGHTS & REFLECTIONS

Bucket List

Date Completed

What I Want To Do:

BUCKET LIST ITEM: #

THOUGHTS & REFLECTIONS

Bucket List

Date Completed

What I Want To Do:

BUCKET LIST ITEM: #

THOUGHTS & REFLECTIONS

Bucket List

Date Completed

What I Want To Do:

BUCKET LIST ITEM: #

THOUGHTS & REFLECTIONS

Bucket List

Date Completed

What I Want To Do:

BUCKET LIST ITEM: #

THOUGHTS & REFLECTIONS

Bucket List

Date Completed

What I Want To Do:

BUCKET LIST ITEM: #

THOUGHTS & REFLECTIONS

Bucket List

Date Completed

What I Want To Do:

BUCKET LIST ITEM: #

THOUGHTS & REFLECTIONS

Bucket List

Date Completed

What I Want To Do:

BUCKET LIST ITEM: #

THOUGHTS & REFLECTIONS

Bucket List

Date Completed

What I Want To Do:

BUCKET LIST ITEM: #

THOUGHTS & REFLECTIONS

Bucket List

Date Completed

What I Want To Do:

BUCKET LIST ITEM: #

THOUGHTS & REFLECTIONS

Bucket List

Date Completed

What I Want To Do:

BUCKET LIST ITEM: #

THOUGHTS & REFLECTIONS

Bucket List

Date Completed

What I Want To Do:

BUCKET LIST ITEM: #

THOUGHTS & REFLECTIONS

Bucket List

Date Completed

What I Want To Do:

BUCKET LIST ITEM: #

THOUGHTS & REFLECTIONS

Bucket List

Date Completed

What I Want To Do:

BUCKET LIST ITEM: #

THOUGHTS & REFLECTIONS

Bucket List

Date Completed

What I Want To Do:

BUCKET LIST ITEM: #

THOUGHTS & REFLECTIONS

Bucket List

Date Completed

What I Want To Do:

BUCKET LIST ITEM: #

THOUGHTS & REFLECTIONS

Bucket List

Date Completed

What I Want To Do:

BUCKET LIST ITEM: #

THOUGHTS & REFLECTIONS

Bucket List

Date Completed

What I Want To Do:

BUCKET LIST ITEM: #

THOUGHTS & REFLECTIONS

Bucket List

Date Completed

What I Want To Do:

BUCKET LIST ITEM: #

THOUGHTS & REFLECTIONS

Bucket List

Date Completed

What I Want To Do:

BUCKET LIST ITEM: #

THOUGHTS & REFLECTIONS

Bucket List

Date Completed

What I Want To Do:

BUCKET LIST ITEM: #

THOUGHTS & REFLECTIONS

Bucket List

Date Completed

What I Want To Do:

BUCKET LIST ITEM: #

THOUGHTS & REFLECTIONS

Bucket List

Date Completed

What I Want To Do:

BUCKET LIST ITEM: #

THOUGHTS & REFLECTIONS

Bucket List

Date Completed

What I Want To Do:

BUCKET LIST ITEM: #

THOUGHTS & REFLECTIONS

Bucket List

Date Completed

What I Want To Do:

BUCKET LIST ITEM: #

THOUGHTS & REFLECTIONS

Bucket List

Date Completed

What I Want To Do:

BUCKET LIST ITEM: #

THOUGHTS & REFLECTIONS

Bucket List

Date Completed

What I Want To Do:

BUCKET LIST ITEM: #

THOUGHTS & REFLECTIONS

Bucket List

Date Completed

What I Want To Do:

BUCKET LIST ITEM: #

THOUGHTS & REFLECTIONS

Bucket List

Date Completed

What I Want To Do:

BUCKET LIST ITEM: #

THOUGHTS & REFLECTIONS

Bucket List

Date Completed

What I Want To Do:

BUCKET LIST ITEM: #

THOUGHTS & REFLECTIONS

Bucket List

Date Completed

What I Want To Do:

BUCKET LIST ITEM: #

THOUGHTS & REFLECTIONS

Bucket List

What I Want To Do:

Date Completed

BUCKET LIST ITEM: #

THOUGHTS & REFLECTIONS

Bucket List

Date Completed

What I Want To Do:

BUCKET LIST ITEM: #

THOUGHTS & REFLECTIONS

Bucket List

Date Completed

What I Want To Do:

BUCKET LIST ITEM: #

THOUGHTS & REFLECTIONS

Bucket List

Date Completed

What I Want To Do:

BUCKET LIST ITEM: #

THOUGHTS & REFLECTIONS

Bucket List

Date Completed

What I Want To Do:

BUCKET LIST ITEM: #

THOUGHTS & REFLECTIONS

Bucket List

Date Completed

What I Want To Do:

BUCKET LIST ITEM: #

THOUGHTS & REFLECTIONS

Bucket List

Date Completed

What I Want To Do:

BUCKET LIST ITEM: #

THOUGHTS & REFLECTIONS

Bucket List

Date Completed

What I Want To Do:

BUCKET LIST ITEM: #

THOUGHTS & REFLECTIONS

Bucket List

Date Completed

What I Want To Do:

BUCKET LIST ITEM: #

THOUGHTS & REFLECTIONS

Bucket List

Date Completed

What I Want To Do:

BUCKET LIST ITEM: #

THOUGHTS & REFLECTIONS

Bucket List

Date Completed

What I Want To Do:

BUCKET LIST ITEM: #

THOUGHTS & REFLECTIONS

Bucket List

Date Completed

What I Want To Do:

BUCKET LIST ITEM: #

THOUGHTS & REFLECTIONS

Bucket List

Date Completed

What I Want To Do:

BUCKET LIST ITEM: #

THOUGHTS & REFLECTIONS

Bucket List

Date Completed

What I Want To Do:

BUCKET LIST ITEM: #

THOUGHTS & REFLECTIONS

Bucket List

Date Completed

What I Want To Do:

BUCKET LIST ITEM: #

THOUGHTS & REFLECTIONS

Bucket List

Date Completed

What I Want To Do:

BUCKET LIST ITEM: #

THOUGHTS & REFLECTIONS

Bucket List

Date Completed

What I Want To Do:

BUCKET LIST ITEM: #

THOUGHTS & REFLECTIONS

Bucket List

Date Completed

What I Want To Do:

BUCKET LIST ITEM: #

THOUGHTS & REFLECTIONS

Bucket List

Date Completed

What I Want To Do:

BUCKET LIST ITEM: #

THOUGHTS & REFLECTIONS

Bucket List

Date Completed

What I Want To Do:

BUCKET LIST ITEM: #

THOUGHTS & REFLECTIONS

Bucket List

Date Completed

What I Want To Do:

BUCKET LIST ITEM: #

THOUGHTS & REFLECTIONS

Bucket List

Date Completed

What I Want To Do:

BUCKET LIST ITEM: #

THOUGHTS & REFLECTIONS

Bucket List

Date Completed

What I Want To Do:

BUCKET LIST ITEM: #

THOUGHTS & REFLECTIONS

Bucket List

Date Completed

What I Want To Do:

BUCKET LIST ITEM: #

THOUGHTS & REFLECTIONS

Bucket List

Date Completed

What I Want To Do:

BUCKET LIST ITEM: #

THOUGHTS & REFLECTIONS

Bucket List

Date Completed

What I Want To Do:

BUCKET LIST ITEM: #

THOUGHTS & REFLECTIONS

Bucket List

Date Completed

What I Want To Do:

BUCKET LIST ITEM: #

THOUGHTS & REFLECTIONS

Bucket List

Date Completed

What I Want To Do:

BUCKET LIST ITEM: #

THOUGHTS & REFLECTIONS

Bucket List

Date Completed

What I Want To Do:

BUCKET LIST ITEM: #

THOUGHTS & REFLECTIONS

Bucket List

Date Completed

What I Want To Do:

BUCKET LIST ITEM: #

THOUGHTS & REFLECTIONS

Bucket List

Date Completed

What I Want To Do:

BUCKET LIST ITEM: #

THOUGHTS & REFLECTIONS

Bucket List

Date Completed

What I Want To Do:

BUCKET LIST ITEM: #

THOUGHTS & REFLECTIONS

Bucket List

Date Completed

What I Want To Do:

BUCKET LIST ITEM: #

THOUGHTS & REFLECTIONS

Bucket List

Date Completed

What I Want To Do:

BUCKET LIST ITEM: #

THOUGHTS & REFLECTIONS

Bucket List

Date Completed

What I Want To Do:

BUCKET LIST ITEM: #

THOUGHTS & REFLECTIONS

Bucket List

Date Completed

What I Want To Do:

BUCKET LIST ITEM: #

THOUGHTS & REFLECTIONS

Bucket List

Date Completed

What I Want To Do:

BUCKET LIST ITEM: #

THOUGHTS & REFLECTIONS

Bucket List

Date Completed

What I Want To Do:

BUCKET LIST ITEM: #

THOUGHTS & REFLECTIONS

Bucket List

Date Completed

What I Want To Do:

BUCKET LIST ITEM: #

THOUGHTS & REFLECTIONS

Bucket List

Date Completed

What I Want To Do:

BUCKET LIST ITEM: #

THOUGHTS & REFLECTIONS

Bucket List

Date Completed

What I Want To Do:

BUCKET LIST ITEM: #

THOUGHTS & REFLECTIONS

Bucket List

Date Completed

What I Want To Do:

BUCKET LIST ITEM: #

THOUGHTS & REFLECTIONS

Bucket List

Date Completed

What I Want To Do:

BUCKET LIST ITEM: #

THOUGHTS & REFLECTIONS

Bucket List

Date Completed

What I Want To Do:

BUCKET LIST ITEM: #

THOUGHTS & REFLECTIONS

Bucket List

Date Completed

What I Want To Do:

BUCKET LIST ITEM: #

THOUGHTS & REFLECTIONS

Bucket List

Date Completed

What I Want To Do:

BUCKET LIST ITEM: #

THOUGHTS & REFLECTIONS

Bucket List

Date Completed

What I Want To Do:

BUCKET LIST ITEM: #

THOUGHTS & REFLECTIONS

Bucket List

Date Completed

What I Want To Do:

BUCKET LIST ITEM: #

THOUGHTS & REFLECTIONS

Bucket List

Date Completed

What I Want To Do:

BUCKET LIST ITEM: #

THOUGHTS & REFLECTIONS

Bucket List

Date Completed

What I Want To Do:

BUCKET LIST ITEM: #

THOUGHTS & REFLECTIONS

Bucket List

Date Completed

What I Want To Do:

BUCKET LIST ITEM: #

THOUGHTS & REFLECTIONS

Bucket List

Date Completed

What I Want To Do:

BUCKET LIST ITEM: #

THOUGHTS & REFLECTIONS

Bucket List

Date Completed

What I Want To Do:

BUCKET LIST ITEM: #

THOUGHTS & REFLECTIONS

Bucket List

Date Completed

What I Want To Do:

BUCKET LIST ITEM: #

THOUGHTS & REFLECTIONS

Bucket List

Date Completed

What I Want To Do:

BUCKET LIST ITEM: #

THOUGHTS & REFLECTIONS

Bucket List

Date Completed

What I Want To Do:

BUCKET LIST ITEM: #

THOUGHTS & REFLECTIONS

Bucket List

What I Want To Do:

Date Completed

BUCKET LIST ITEM: #

THOUGHTS & REFLECTIONS

Bucket List

Date Completed

What I Want To Do:

BUCKET LIST ITEM: #

THOUGHTS & REFLECTIONS

Made in the USA
Monee, IL
28 July 2021